GIANTS OF THE OLD TESTAMENT

LESSONS ON LIVING FROM

MOSES

Becoming a Light in the Darkness

A devotional by

WOODROW KROLL

D1059190

BACK TO THE BIBLE ®
Lincoln, Nebraska

CONTENTS

DAY 1

Exodus 4:31

*So the people believed;
and when they heard that
the LORD had visited the children of Israel
and that He had looked on their affliction,
then they bowed their heads
and worshiped.*

When Nothing Else Will Do

There are times when it seems the only appropriate thing to do is worship. Kenneth Grahame, in his children's book *The Wind in the Willows,* describes such a time. Mole and Rat had been out searching for a lost child. In their search they came to a part of the river that they hadn't visited before and found themselves in the commanding presence of the Piper. "Then suddenly the Mole felt a great awe fall upon him, an awe that turned his muscles to water, bowed his head, and rooted his feet to the ground. . . 'Rat!' he found breath to whisper, shaking, 'Are you afraid?' 'Afraid?' murmured the Rat, his eyes shinning with unutterable love, 'Afraid? Of Him? O, never, never! And yet—and yet—O, Mole, I am afraid!' Then the two animals, crouching to the earth, bowed their heads and did worship."

When the Israelites heard and saw all

4

that Moses and Aaron had to share (vv. 29-30), they, too, were overcome with wonder. The God of the universe was concerned about them and they "bowed their heads and worshiped." There was nothing more appropriate that they could do.

God is still the same wondrous Person today as He was then. He is more powerful than we can ever imagine. He rules all of creation and has done so since eternity past. Every living thing draws its life from Him and owes its continued existence to Him. Compared to Him, we are like the Rat and the Mole, pummeled with a feeling of insignificance. Yet He loves us so much that He gave His only begotten Son to redeem us from our sins.

Take time today to meditate on God's awesomeness. Let the wonder of His love fill you with astonishment. Allow the realization of His concern for every aspect of your life to wash over you in amazement. Then bow your head and worship.

Those who truly know God will truly worship Him.

Reflections/Prayer Requests

DAY 2

Exodus 5:1-2

*Afterward Moses and Aaron
went in and told Pharaoh,
"Thus says the LORD God of Israel:
'Let My people go, that they may
hold a feast to Me in the wilderness.'"
And Pharaoh said, "Who is the LORD,
that I should obey His voice to let Israel go?
I do not know the LORD, nor will I let Israel go."*

Who Is the Lord?

Ignorance can be costly. During the War of 1812, between the United States and Great Britain, the Americans crossed the Canadian border and destroyed York. The British retaliated by burning Washington, D.C. Finally, on December 24, 1814, representatives of the two countries met in Belgium and signed the Treaty of Ghent.

Unfortunately, the news of the peace was delayed, and on January 8, 1815, the two opposing armies met in the Battle of New Orleans. More than 2,000 men lost their lives in a needless battle because they were ignorant of the peace treaty.

Pharaoh also paid a costly price for his ignorance. Even though Egypt had many gods, they were ignorant of the one true God. When confronted with God's command, Pharaoh arrogantly demanded,

"Who is the LORD, that I should obey His voice to let Israel go?" Over the next several months, he came to know God only too well as He brought plague after plague upon the land until His voice was heeded. The loss of their cattle, their crops and their firstborn children became part of the price the Egyptians paid for their ignorance.

Ignorance is still costly. Many people will go into an eternal hell because they are ignorant of the plan of salvation. Others will experience heartbreak and failure because they are ignorant of God's design for the family or for the biblical use of personal finances.

Don't settle for ignorance. Educate yourself in the will and ways of God. Study the Bible and apply it diligently. The cost of ignorance is too high, especially when ignorance can be avoided.

When it comes to knowing the Lord, ignorance is not bliss.

Reflections/Prayer Requests

_____

_____

_____

_____

DAY 3

Exodus 5:4, 8

*Then the king of Egypt said to them,
"Moses and Aaron, why do you take the
people from their work? Get back to your labor."*

*"And you shall lay on them the quota of bricks
which they made before. You shall not reduce it.
For they are idle; therefore they cry out, saying,
'Let us go and sacrifice to our God.'"*

No Time for God

A church in Minnesota found itself in trouble with the courts. A family in the church who faithfully tithed for years suddenly went bankrupt through no fault of their own. The bankruptcy courts determined that all the money this family had tithed to the church during the previous year should be returned to help settle outstanding debts. The logic the court system followed was that the family had not received anything of value in return for their gifts. The final outcome of this dispute will be years in the settling, but it reflects an attitude that is common today: if our efforts do not result in a tangible product, they are of no value.

Pharaoh felt the same way. His concern was producing bricks. Some identify the Pharaoh of Moses' time as Ramses II, who

8

ruled for 66 years and built many towns, temples and monuments. Whoever the Pharaoh of the Exodus was, he was concerned more with bricks and mortar than with the spiritual life of his slaves. The fact that the Israelites had time to think about spiritual matters indicated to him that they had too much time on their hands. His solution was to give them more to do so they would have no opportunity for such unproductive activities as worship.

Many people today see time spent in spiritual pursuits as a waste. They have no time for such unproductive indulgences.

Let us remember that man was created for fellowship with God. He wants to spend intimate time with us. When we're too busy for God, we're busier than God intended for us to be.

Carve out some quality time to spend with God today.

Time with God is invested—not spent.

Reflections/Prayer Requests

_____

_____

_____

_____

DAY 4

Exodus 5:21

*And they said to them,
"Let the L*ORD* look on you and judge,
because you have made us
abhorrent in the sight of Pharaoh
and in the sight of his servants,
to put a sword in their hand to kill us."*

Life Isn't Fair

Abraham Lincoln was one of the most criticized U.S. presidents ever to hold the office. He was at various times called a fool, a fraud and, by virtue of his long arms and legs, an ape. His most famous speech, the Gettysburg Address, was dismissed at the time as "the silly remarks of the President" and thought best that "the veil of oblivion be dropped over them and they no more be repeated or thought of." It was only with the benefit of hindsight that Americans realized he was one of the greatest presidents in our nation's history.

Moses also came in for his share of unfair criticism. After Pharaoh informed the Jewish officials that they would be given no more straw and yet be expected to keep up with their quota of bricks, these men vented their anger on Moses. "This is all your fault," they said. "You have given Pharaoh the reason he wanted to work us to death."

They totally ignored the fact that Pharaoh had been increasing their work load to an almost unbearable level anyway. In their eyes it was all the fault of this troublemaker from the backside of the desert and his brother. It is only the judgment of history that has proven them wrong.

Criticism is a natural part of the leadership package, but that doesn't make it any easier to bear—especially if it seems unfair. If you are the object of unfair criticism, take heart. Remember that history has often proven wrong the most strident critics. Give the sting of that criticism over to God and rest in His affirming love. After all, He is the only One whose opinion really counts. If He approves of what you're doing, don't lose any sleep over those who criticize you wrongly. God will make all things right.

It doesn't make any difference who is for you or who is against you as long as God is with you.

Reflections/Prayer Requests

_____

_____

_____

_____

DAY 5

Exodus 5:22

So Moses returned to the LORD and said, "Lord, why have You brought trouble on this people? Why is it You have sent me?"

Doubting in the Dark

Many people find driving at night disorienting. Routes that are effortlessly navigated during the daylight hours seem twisted and turned around at night. Landmarks that are readily recognized before the sun goes down take on a new appearance in the dark. It is easy for these people to get confused and begin to doubt if they are even going in the right direction.

Moses experienced a similar time of confusion and doubt. He became disoriented in the midst of spiritual darkness and could not see God's direction. It seemed the more he called for Pharaoh to let his people go, the more difficult their lives became. Rather than letting the people go free, Pharaoh laid even heavier burdens upon them. Instead of being a blessing to the Israelites, Moses started to think he was a curse. He began to doubt if he had clearly understood what God intended for him to do.

Perhaps you are experiencing that same confusion today. You believe you are doing what God wants you to do, but the situation is getting worse instead of better. If so, do what Moses did. He went back to God for clarification and assurance. He asked, "Why is it You have sent me?"

It never hurts to recheck our spiritual directions. Go back to the Bible and see if your actions are consistent with the Word. Seek God in prayer and ask Him to reveal if you've perhaps misunderstood His desire for you. If you find that you are missing the mark, ask God to help you make whatever corrections are necessary. If you're on target, continue to follow Moses' example— keep moving forward and trust God with the results.

What God has revealed in the light should never be doubted in the dark.

Reflections/Prayer Requests

DAY 6

Exodus 6:2-3

*And God spoke to Moses and said to him:
"I am the LORD. I appeared to Abraham,
to Isaac, and to Jacob, as God Almighty,
but by My name LORD I was not
known to them."*

The Longer I Serve Him

C. B. Moss wrote, "We do not believe that God has added, or ever will add, anything to His revelation in His Son. But we can now see many things in that revelation which could not be seen by those who first received it."

When God revealed Himself to Moses, He was the same God who had appeared to Abraham, Isaac and Jacob as "God Almighty" (El-Shaddai). But now He was revealing His character as LORD (Yahweh or Jehovah). The name LORD carries the sense of being a covenant keeper. Not that this name had never been used before, but now God was demonstrating His covenant character in a deeper, more personal way. God had made numerous promises to Abraham, Isaac and Jacob: to make them a nation (Gen. 12:2), to provide a land for them to possess (v. 7) and to bring them out of Egypt (50:24). Now it was time for Him to keep those promises. Through Moses He

14

would reveal Himself to be the Lord, the promise keeper.

The longer we walk with the Lord, the more He reveals Himself to us. He who began as a Savior also will reveal Himself as a trustworthy Friend. He who is our trustworthy Friend also will reveal Himself as our Guide. And He who is our Guide will be our Comforter as well.

An impoverished woman was taken to the seashore by some of her neighbors. As she stared at the seemingly endless stretch of water, she said, "Finally, I've seen something that there's enough of." The same is true of God. There is always something more to know and experience in Him. He is a boundless source of new understanding. No wonder the songwriter exclaims, "The longer I serve Him, the sweeter He grows."

The longer you serve God, the more you'll understand why.

Reflections/Prayer Requests

_____

_____

_____

_____

_____

Exodus 6:9

So Moses spoke thus to the children of Israel; but they did not heed Moses, because of anguish of spirit and cruel bondage.

The Trouble With Trouble

An old fable says that Satan once held a sale and offered all the tools of his profession to anyone who would pay the price. They were spread out on the table and each one labeled: hatred, malice, envy, despair, sickness, sensuality—the weapons we all know so well. But off to one side lay a harmless-looking instrument marked "discouragement." It was old and worn, but it was priced far above all the rest. When asked the reason why, the devil replied, "Because I can use this one so much more easily than the others. No one knows that it belongs to me, so with it I can open doors that are tightly bolted against the others."

Satan had certainly gotten inside the camp of the Israelites. They were totally discouraged. Moses had confronted Pharaoh, but instead of the deliverance they had been promised, they were experiencing even more cruel and unreasonable afflictions. Moses, whom they thought had been sent by God, seemed powerless before Pharaoh. Consequently, not only were the people discouraged, they became disobedient. They chose to no longer heed Moses' advice.

Many Christians find that being obedient to God does not make life easier for them. Often standing up for the truth of God's Word makes us the object of people's ridicule and even persecution.

Don't be discouraged if afflictions come your way. This makes you part of a great and glorious cloud of witnesses who have experienced the same thing. And whatever you do, don't back away from your duty as a Christian just because you may experience difficulty. Ask God to show you how you can turn these afflictions into blessings for others and praise for Him. He did it for Moses; He'll do it for you.

Brooding on your troubles only hatches discouragement.

Reflections/Prayer Requests

_____

_____

_____

_____

_____

_____

DAY 8

Exodus 6:12, 30

And Moses spoke before the LORD, saying,
"The children of Israel have not heeded me.
How then shall Pharaoh heed me,
for I am of uncircumcised lips?"

But Moses said before the LORD,
"Behold, I am of uncircumcised lips,
and how shall Pharaoh heed me?"

They Said It Couldn't Be Done

In 1870 a bishop was greatly incensed when it was suggested that man might some day fly. He strenuously argued that such an idea was blasphemous, declaring, "Don't you know that flight is reserved for angels?" The bishop's name was Milton Wright. On December 17, 1903, his two sons, Orville and Wilbur, flew the first airplane at Kittyhawk, North Carolina. What couldn't be done in some folks' opinion was indeed accomplished.

Moses was convinced that his faltering lips could never persuade Pharaoh to let the Israelites go. But God said, "Go and speak," so Moses did. Despite all his shortcomings, Moses found that what he thought could not possibly be done was exactly done, with God's help. Pharaoh finally let the people go.

Many people are quick to tell you something can't be done. On the surface it may appear that way. Perhaps it does seem impossible for your loved one to come to Christ, or for a situation at work to change, or for a relationship to be mended. But God says, "Behold, I am the LORD, the God of all flesh. Is there anything too hard for Me?" (Jer. 32:27). Of course not—nothing is impossible with God. Our responsibility is to trust and obey, not to doubt and despair.

The next time someone says to you, "It can't be done!" remind them that they are not the first to feel that way, and they are not the first to be wrong. For God, nothing is too difficult.

The word **impossible** *is not in God's vocabulary.*

Reflections/Prayer Requests

_____

_____

_____

_____

_____

_____

_____

DAY 9

Exodus 7:6-7

Then Moses and Aaron did so;
just as the LORD commanded them,
so they did. And Moses was eighty years old
and Aaron eighty-three years old
when they spoke to Pharaoh.

It's Never Too Late

Usefulness doesn't have to stop at retirement. At age 89 architect Philip Johnson designed a New York skyscraper with gold-tinted glass. Critics are hailing it as a masterpiece. At 92 theater caricaturist Al Hirschfield attends every Broadway opening and puts in seven days a week at his drawing board. Poet Stanley Kunitz won the 1995 National Book Award at age 90. These men have not allowed age to stand in the way of usefulness. They know it's never too late to be productive.

God also uses those who are skiing the downhill side of life. Moses was 80 when he was called to his greatest task and Aaron was 83. In fact, God would use them for the next 40 years to lead the people of Israel. Certainly there must have been younger men to fill the role, but God chose Moses, who was picked at birth and seasoned by years. In God's sight it's not your age that counts; it's your willingness to obey His call.

If you're part of the younger generation, be careful how you view God's older saints. Age is not the critical success factor; availability and obedience are.

If you're one of those who needs the fire department to stand by when you light the candles on your birthday cake, don't be too ready to settle into a rocking chair. Saints who no longer are saddled with a daily job can serve in fruitful ways that others can't. Volunteer to work in the church office, visit shut-ins or encourage those who are in the hospital.

The mission field is another area that can use a lift from senior saints. Many missionaries could use help in accomplishing their goals. If you're a retired teacher, printer, mechanic, nurse or whatever, your most exciting days of ministry may be ahead of you. Open up your life to God's possibilities.

God doesn't look at the calendar; He looks at the heart.

Reflections/Prayer Requests

_____

_____

_____

_____

DAY 10

Exodus 7:11-12

*But Pharaoh also called
the wise men and the sorcerers;
so the magicians of Egypt, they also did
in like manner with their enchantments.
For every man threw down his rod,
and they became serpents.
But Aaron's rod swallowed up their rods.*

Master Deceiver

Larry Wu-Tai Chin was a master of deception. For nearly 30 years, Chin, 63, a naturalized American citizen, lived a double life. While working as a highly valued translator and analyst for the CIA, he also passed classified documents to the People's Republic of China. Throughout his four-day trial, Chin insisted that he had only intended to improve relations between his homeland and his adopted country. Nevertheless, he became the first American to be convicted of spying for China.

The world is filled with all kinds of deception. Pharaoh's magicians were copycat deceivers. Some suggest these sorcerers knew just where to grasp the neck of a serpent to apply pressure and cause it to become rigid. This would give it the appearance of a staff until the snake was released. The lack of true power behind this trick, however, was evidenced when Aaron's rod swallowed up all the others.

None of these tricksters, though, can compare to Satan. He is the master deceiver. Since the time of Adam and Eve he has beguiled men and women into believing that they could live apart from God and be happy. How many people do you know who have been lured into a lifetime of vanity and misery through his craftiness?

Christians must remember that the best protection against Satan's deception is God's truthfulness, as found in His Holy Word. Like Aaron's rod, God's truth will swallow up the falsehoods of the Evil One. Make it a daily habit to read and study your Bible. Ask the Holy Spirit to be your teacher and guide to the truth of the Scriptures and the deceptions of Satan. For optimum protection, know both your Bible and your enemy.

Satan's tricks are no match for God's truths.

Reflections/Prayer Requests

_____

_____

_____

_____

DAY 11

Exodus 7:17-18

Thus says the Lord:
"By this you shall know that I am the Lord.
Behold, I will strike the waters which are in
the river with the rod that is in my hand,
and they shall be turned to blood.

"And the fish that are in the river shall die,
the river shall stink, and the Egyptians will
loathe to drink the water of the river."

Sin Stinks

Humans experience the sensation we identify as smell because we have about 20 million nerve fibers embedded in the lining of our upper nasal passage. As air enters the nose, it carries gaseous molecules over these receptors causing us to identify various odors. Some people have such a keen sense of smell that they can identify other people and even locations by smell without any need for other clues.

Unfortunately, when it comes to sin most people aren't nearly as discriminating. We don't have the "nose" to sniff out sin as we ought. Yet sin does stink. As the dead fish from the Nile began to rot in the hot Egyptian sun, the revolting stench was so strong that the whole river was tainted. The Egyptians couldn't bear to even draw water from it for drinking. The stink from the bloody Nile became an odorous reminder of how sin smells to God.

The prophet Joel also reminds us of this truth when he described the atrocities of an enemy army by saying, "his stench will come up, and his foul odor will rise, because he has done monstrous things" (2:20). Sin always produces a nauseating scent to those who can discern it.

Just imagine how reluctantly we would respond to sin if it smelled the same way to us as it does to God. If you want to please God, ask Him to give you a sensitive sense of smell when it comes to sin. May it not only appear repulsive, may it also smell repugnant.

You'll never revel in sin if it repulses you.

Reflections/Prayer Requests

_____

_____

_____

_____

_____

_____

_____

DAY 12

Exodus 8:13-14

So the LORD did according to the word of Moses. And the frogs died out of the houses, out of the courtyards, and out of the fields. They gathered them together in heaps, and the land stank.

Frog Residue

Natural consequences are often the best form of discipline. A friend of mine had a little daughter who insisted on eating her soap at bath time. Repeated warnings only heightened her delight at nibbling on this odd delicacy. Finally, after being assured that no permanent harm would come to his daughter, Dad let her have her way. She blew bubbles for hours after her bath, but she never ate soap again.

The Egyptians also experienced the consequence of their stubbornness. When Pharaoh refused to let God's people go, He sent a plague of frogs on the land. To make matters worse, Pharaoh's magicians worked their "magic" to give the people a double dose of frog legs. Even Pharaoh finally had enough and asked for the frogs to be removed in return for the release of the Israelites.

When Moses interceded for the Egyptians, however, God did not remove the frogs. Instead, He caused them to die. That cured one problem and created another. In a matter of hours the land was filled with stinking piles of frogs—the residue of the people's willful sin.

Sin often leaves a residue in a Christian's life too. Even though a sin might be forgiven, God may well allow the consequences to continue. He does not do this to exact revenge, but to remind us of the seriousness of sin. The natural consequences of our behavior are often God's way of discouraging us from repeating that behavior in the future.

When tempted to sin, do not be lulled by Satan's assurance that you can be forgiven. That is true, but remember Pharaoh's frog residue. The sin may be forgiven and forgotten, but the consequences may follow you into eternity.

If you don't want the fruits of sin, stay out of the devil's garden.

Reflections/Prayer Requests

_____

_____

_____

DAY 13

Exodus 8:16, 19

Then the LORD said to Moses,
"Say to Aaron, 'Stretch out your staff,
and strike the dust of the earth,
so that it may become gnats
throughout all the land of Egypt.'"

Then the magicians said to Pharaoh,
"This is the finger of God." (NASB)

One-digit Demolition

The Loizeaux family offers a unique service. As owners of Controlled Demolition Inc., they developed a technique for demolishing buildings by applying small amounts of dynamite to the structural supports. A single detonation causes even the largest building to implode into a dusty heap of rubble with minimum effect on surrounding structures.

Pharaoh's magicians found that God was equally capable. When Aaron struck the dust of the ground, God caused it to become gnats. This was something the magicians were unable to duplicate. Furthermore, these vexing, almost-invisible insects interfered with the ritual purity of the priests, preventing them from fulfilling their duties to their gods. Unable to replicate the miracle and unable to tolerate the consequences of these minuscule but mighty pests, the priestly magicians finally admitted to Pharaoh, "This is the finger of God."

With a single digit of His powerful hand, God brought the whole land of Egypt to its knees. Their belief in the powerful arm of their gods lay in shambles. God proved He had more power in one finger than all their idols put together.

When life seems overwhelming and worries rise up like towering skyscrapers, remember that God only needs to point a finger to bring it all tumbling down. Bring your troubles to Him and leave them there. He'll take care of them. Remember, He is the master of the one-digit demolition.

God can do with one finger what others cannot do with all their resources.

Reflections/Prayer Requests

_____

_____

_____

_____

_____

_____

_____

DAY 14

Exodus 8:25, 28

*Then Pharaoh called for Moses
and Aaron, and said, "Go, sacrifice to
your God in the land."*

*And Pharaoh said,
"I will let you go, that you may sacrifice
to the LORD your God in the wilderness;
only you shall not go very far away.
Intercede for me."*

No Holding Back

During the 12th century, military expeditions were launched to retake the Holy Land from Muslim conquerors. The crusaders often hired soldiers of fortune to fight alongside them, but because it was a "holy" war they required these mercenaries to be baptized before fighting. While meeting this requirement, however, these soldiers-for-hire would hold their weapons out of the water to indicate that they retained the freedom to do with them whatever they wanted. They were willing to submit to some things, but not to all.

After several devastating plagues, Pharaoh, too, was finally willing to go part way with God. He gave permission for the Israelites to halt their work and carry out their sacrifices, but they must only sacrifice "in the land." Yet this was not what God had commanded. Moses told Pharaoh the people needed to go "three days'" journey from Egypt (v. 27), but the stubborn ruler insisted that they "not go very far away."

Pharaoh had not learned what many Christians also have not learned: when it comes to obedience, God wants nothing held back. Partial obedience is still disobedience.

Is there an area in your life that you are withholding from God? Does God have the complete management of your finances? Does He have the total control of your social life? Are you willing to let Him decide where you live, what career you choose and whom you marry? Either we obey God completely, in every area of our lives, or we have not obeyed Him at all. Give yourself to Him, all that you are and all that you have. God always rewards those who abandon themselves in obedience to Him.

Partial obedience is just another name for disobedience.

Reflections/Prayer Requests

DAY 15

Exodus 8:28, 32

*And Pharaoh said, "I will let you go,
that you may sacrifice to the LORD your God in
the wilderness; only you shall not go
very far away. Intercede for me."*

*But Pharaoh hardened his heart at this time
also; neither would he let the people go.*

Dishonest Dealings

Americans are in the midst of an honesty crisis. Some call our era the "Age of the Rip-off." Employee theft is nearly one billion dollars a week. Twenty percent of the gross national product goes unreported to the government. Some 24 percent of respondents to a *Money* magazine survey said they would keep the cash if they found a wallet containing $1,000.

Pharaoh also had a problem with honesty. With each new crisis he would promise to let the people go. But when the critical moment of a plague was past, he would renege on his promise. Such dishonesty eventually cost him the life of all the firstborn children of Egypt.

Honesty is an essential ingredient in a Christian's life. At age 24, Abraham Lincoln was paid an annual salary of $55.70 to serve as the postmaster of New Salem,

Illinois. The New Salem post office closed in 1836, but it took several years before an agent arrived to settle accounts. When all the records were balanced, the agent claimed that $17 was due the government. Lincoln crossed the room, opened an old trunk and took out a yellow cotton rag. Untying it, he spread out the cloth and there was the $17. Honest Abe had reserved it untouched for all those years.

While as a Christian you may not deliberately steal or lie, what about other opportunities for dishonesty? Do you stretch your coffee break beyond the allotted time? Do you make promises and then break them? Are you careless with items loaned to you? These are all forms of dishonesty. Pray that God would reveal any area of your life in which you are not living up to His expectations.

It says a lot about our society when the word honesty *has to be preceded by* old-fashioned.

Reflections/Prayer Requests

_____

_____

_____

_____

DAY 16

Exodus 9:2-4

*For if you refuse to let them go,
and still hold them, behold, the hand of
the L*ORD *will be on your cattle in the field,
on the horses, on the donkeys, on the camels,
on the oxen, and on the sheep; a very severe
pestilence. And the L*ORD *will make
a difference between the livestock of Israel
and the livestock of Egypt. So nothing shall die
of all that belongs to the children of Israel.*

It Makes a Difference

In his book *None of These Diseases*, Dr. S. I. McMillen offers evidence that when we not only know God but obey Him as well, it makes a positive difference in our lives physically, emotionally and spiritually. God's commandments are not given to be a burden but to help us live more fulfilling lives. When it comes to the practical art of living, God makes a real difference between obedient believers and the rest of the world.

The Egyptians discovered this the hard way. When they refused to obey God and allow the people of Israel to leave, a severe disease decimated their livestock. The animals that belonged to God's people, however, were unharmed.

This is not to say that God always puts a protective bubble over His people. As part of a fallen world, we share in many of the same trials and tribulations as everyone else. However, some of those trials are a consequence of disobedience. For example, doctors at Johns Hopkins University concluded that women are 5 to 11 times more likely to develop cervical cancer if their husbands frequent prostitutes. The spread of AIDS is also often linked to promiscuous sexuality. Many life-shattering diseases could be avoided simply by obeying God's Word.

God desires a wonderful life for you. His commandments are given for your protection, not for your detriment. They are to increase the quality of your life, not decrease it. Rejoice that you have a God who cares enough to make a difference.

When you try to break God's commandments, you only break yourself.

Reflections/Prayer Requests

_____

_____

_____

_____

_____

DAY 17

Exodus 9:8-9

*So the L*ORD *said to Moses and Aaron,
"Take for yourselves handfuls of ashes from a
furnace, and let Moses scatter it toward the
heavens in the sight of Pharaoh. And it will
become fine dust in all the land of Egypt, and it
will cause boils that break out in sores on man
and beast throughout all the land of Egypt."*

Ashes From the Furnace

The Greeks believed in a legendary bird
called the Phoenix. It had brilliant gold and
reddish-purple feathers and was as large as
an eagle. Some claimed that the Phoenix
lived for exactly 500 years and at the end of
that time burned itself on a funeral pyre.
Out of the ashes, however, a new Phoenix
rose with renewed youth and beauty.

Like the Phoenix, God can take ashes
and bring forth something marvelous and
wonderful. For Moses and Aaron He used
the ashes from a furnace to remind
Pharaoh that he was not as powerful as he
thought. When the winds spread the ashes
over the land of Egypt, boils broke out on
all the people. Even the court magicians
were unable to stand on their feet. They
quickly discovered what the God of Israel
was able to do with something as seeming-

ly useless as ashes.

The fiery furnace of trials and afflictions also can leave our lives in ashes. When all our hopes and plans are burned up, it may seem that nothing is left except useless residue. Yet if we give God the ashes, He is able to bring out of them a whole new life purified and sanctified to His service.

Does it seem that all your dreams have gone up in smoke? Don't discard those ashes. Give what's left to God and watch the divine wonder of His ability to bring beauty from ashes.

In God's hands, even ashes have a purpose.

Reflections/Prayer Requests

_____

_____

_____

_____

_____

_____

_____

_____

_____

DAY 18

Exodus 9:18-19

*Behold, tomorrow about this time I will cause
very heavy hail to rain down, such as has not
been in Egypt since its founding until now.
Therefore send now and gather your livestock
and all that you have in the field, for the hail
shall come down on every man and every
animal which is found in the field and
is not brought home; and they shall die.*

Warning: Trouble Ahead

The Wall Street Journal exposed an elaborate conspiracy to swindle nonprofit ministries by a group called New Era Philanthropy. The New Era president promised to double an investor's money in only six months. Many Christian and other nonprofit groups had invested millions with New Era when the scheme collapsed. They found themselves in bankruptcy court faced with enormous losses. This happened despite the fact that some financial advisors warned them against it. The warnings mostly fell on deaf ears because the deal seemed too good to pass up.

When God brings judgment, He also provides a warning. Unfortunately, it often falls on deaf ears. The Egyptians were warned that a horrendous hail storm would be fatal to every unprotected man and animal. Some heeded the warning, but the majority did not. The loss of human lives and livestock was devastating.

Even today God often prefaces His judgments with warnings. For almost 2,000 years He has warned man that "the wages of sin is death" (Rom. 6:23). He also has warned that we will be held accountable for the "deeds of the flesh" whether we are a Christian (2 Cor. 5:10) or not (Rev. 20:13).

God gets no pleasure out of catching people unawares. Sixteen times the New Testament admonishes, "Let him hear." God takes great delight when people heed His warnings and save themselves grief. Be sure that your spiritual ears are attune to God's warnings. That way you'll always know when there's trouble ahead, and avoid it.

God would rather you gave heed than get hurt.

Reflections/Prayer Requests

DAY 19

Exodus 9:20

*He who feared the word of the LORD
among the servants of Pharaoh made his
servants and his livestock flee to the houses.*

Cracks in the Armor

Ancient soldiers were well protected by
their armor. They had a round shield or
buckler, a helmet made of metal or leather,
and a breastplate of scale-like plates of
bronze sewn onto cloth or leather. This
made the soldier nearly invincible. Still,
there were often gaps or cracks where the
pieces came together. A skillful archer
could penetrate such cracks with an arrow
and bring his enemy down.

Pharaoh appeared as invincible as a soldier. His word was law and he had all the
resources of mighty Egypt to make sure his
will was enforced. But cracks began to
show in the solid support he had enjoyed
in the past. As plague after plague battered
the land, some of Pharaoh's most loyal
subjects began to take seriously God's
warnings. Invincible as Pharaoh seemed,
God's arrows were finding their mark.

William Wilberforce struggled for many
years against England's involvement in the
slave trade. When he first brought this con-

cern to the floor of parliament, he was heckled to the point that he was forced to take his seat. Before he sat down, however, he declared, "There is coming a day when you will hear me gladly." That day came in 1833 shortly before his death. God's arrow found the crack. The English slave trade was abolished.

Do your problems appear as big and invincible as Pharaoh? Do they face you dressed in armor that seems to turn away all your puny attempts to destroy them? Always remember: You face no problems that don't have a crack in their armor somewhere. At the right time God will send an arrow that will bring them down in defeat. You can count on it!

Trust God; His arrows always find the crack.

Reflections/Prayer Requests

DAY 20

Exodus 9:34-35

*And when Pharaoh saw that the rain,
the hail, and the thunder had ceased,
he sinned yet more; and he hardened
his heart, he and his servants. So the heart
of Pharaoh was hard; neither would he let
the children of Israel go, as the LORD
had spoken by Moses.*

A Matter of Expedience

When the luxury liner *Titanic* first struck an iceberg, men who had been cursing and rolling dice at the gaming tables suddenly fell to their knees in repentant prayer. In a few moments the captain of the ship came on the intercom assuring everyone that the accident was not serious. Survivors related that these same men got up and returned to their cursing and gambling. Obviously their repentance was only for expediency.

Pharaoh had the same attitude. When God sent a plague of hail on the land (vv. 23-24), Pharaoh was ready to admit that he had sinned and that he and his people were wicked (v. 27). In an apparent change of heart, he readily agreed to let the Israelites go. As soon as the hail ceased, however, he hardened his heart and reneged on his agreement.

Many people still use religion the same way. They promise to go to church every Sunday, give 10 percent of their income and cease their evil habits, if only God would deliver them from some difficult problem. But when the crisis is over, so is their commitment. They must not be fooled; God is not deceived. He may get these people out of trouble, but unless they keep their promises greater judgment may come upon them later.

God wants to do so much more for you than offer a quick fix for a temporary problem. He wants to give you a long-term relationship that will bring you eternal joy and fulfillment. God never plays games with you. All His promises are "Yes, and in Him Amen" (2 Cor. 1:20). If you choose to deal sincerely with God, He will deal sincerely with you.

Never make obedience a matter of expedience.

Reflections/Prayer Requests

_____

_____

_____

_____

DAY 21

Exodus 10:3-4

So Moses and Aaron came in to Pharaoh and said to him, "Thus says the Lord God of the Hebrews: 'How long will you refuse to humble yourself before Me? Let My people go, that they may serve Me. Or else, if you refuse to let My people go, behold, tomorrow I will bring locusts into your territory.'"

A Humble Spirit

Years ago a young artist submitted one of his works to be hung in a prestigious art exhibit, but the selection committee rejected it. One of its members, the renowned landscape painter Joseph Turner, insisted that they include the young man's work. The others denied his plea, saying that there was simply no room for it. Turner said no more but quietly removed one of his own pictures, replacing it with the budding artist's. It was an act of humility that the young man never forgot.

Pharaoh didn't have the character of Joseph Turner. He was the most powerful man in Egypt. In fact, he was worshiped as a man-god. According to Egyptian mythology, he was the descendent of Ra, the sun god. His will was not to be contested or his decisions questioned. Understandably, this would not breed humility. The lack of a humble spirit, however, brought great anguish not only to Pharaoh, but to those around him as well.

God places a high premium on a humble spirit. Psalm 147:6 says, "The LORD lifts up the humble." But the psalmist also says, "The one who has a haughty look and a proud heart, Him I will not endure" (101:5).

Humble yourself before God. Let Him have His way in every area of your life. He will exalt you far higher than you could ever climb on your own.

When it comes to humility, neither race, face nor place is important.

Reflections/Prayer Requests

_____

_____

_____

_____

_____

_____

_____

_____

_____

DAY 22

Exodus 10:21-22

*Then the LORD said to Moses,
"Stretch out your hand toward heaven, that
there may be darkness over the land of Egypt,
darkness which may even be felt."
So Moses stretched out his hand toward
heaven, and there was thick darkness
in all the land of Egypt three days.*

Walking in the Light

The *Guiness Book of Records* says that the greatest power failure in history struck seven northeastern states in the United States and Ontario, Canada, on November 9-10, 1965. Approximately 30 million people in an area of about 80,000 square miles were plunged into darkness. Parts of New York City were without electricity for more than 13 hours.

But the *Guiness* record is a Johnny-come-lately. In the days of Moses the whole land of Egypt was immersed in a darkness so thick that it could be felt. That darkness lasted for 72 hours.

Yet even this pales to insignificance when compared to the spiritual darkness that envelops the world today. At least 12 million people in the United States alone believe that their lives can be influenced by the arrangement of the stars and planets.

Advertisements for psychic readings are commonplace on television. There are more spiritist healers in Paris than medical doctors, priests and pastors combined. Europe is the only continent where the church is growing more slowly than the population.

How wonderful to know that Christ can provide light, even in dark days like ours. The illumination of His Word shows you how to live. The radiance of His love rescues you from hopelessness. The glow of His joy keeps you from the darkness of despair. While the world staggers on in darkness, as a Christian you can walk confidently in the light.

If you're tired of living in the darkness, take a first step toward the Light. The Light of the world is Jesus. He will be the Light of your life, too, if you ask Him.

Why stumble in the dark when you can stroll in the Light?

Reflections/Prayer Requests

_____

_____

_____

_____

_____

DAY 23

Exodus 11:2-3

*"Speak now in the hearing of the people,
and let every man ask from his neighbor
and every woman from her neighbor,
articles of silver and articles of gold."
And the L*ORD *gave the people favor in
the sight of the Egyptians. Moreover the
man Moses was very great in
the land of Egypt, in the sight of
Pharaoh's servants and in
the sight of the people.*

Justice at Last

One has to wonder about the justice system in the United States. Georgia Supreme Court Justice Charles L. Weltner observed, "Right now a person who has been through the system and is contemplating a crime probably views things as follows: (1) If I do it I won't get caught; (2) If I get caught I won't get prosecuted; (3) If I get prosecuted I won't get convicted; (4) If I get convicted I won't go to prison; (5) If I go to prison it won't be for very long."

God's justice system, on the other hand, is never misguided. As His people prepared to leave Egypt, God knew that they had been treated unfairly. For 400 years they served their Egyptian masters with no recompense. Therefore, God instructed each family member to ask for articles of silver and gold from their Egyptian tormentors. By this means God not only brought judgment on the Egyptians, He also provided restitution for the Israelites. Justice was finally accomplished, even though from a human perspective it took a while.

If you are experiencing an unjust situation, if you are being taken advantage of, be assured that God is aware of it. You also can be certain He will bring about a just solution, the right solution, at the right time. Don't let injustice defeat you. Instead, rest in God's justice. It may grind slowly, but it grinds very thoroughly. It will grind for you.

With God, justice delayed is not justice denied.

Reflections/Prayer Requests

DAY 24

Exodus 12:7

*"And they shall take some of the blood
[of the lamb] and put it on the two doorposts
and on the lintel of the houses
where they eat it."*

Protected by the Blood

Blood is essential for human life. A speck of blood the size of the dot over the letter "i" contains five million red cells. These are the ones that carry oxygen to the rest of the body. Such a dot also would contain 7,000 white cells. Equipped with deadly chemical arsenals, these cells patrol our bodies to battle any harmful agents that might try to invade. The third element in blood is platelets. This same speck of blood contains about 300,000 of these mobile first-aid kits. They rush to the scene of an accident to seal breaks in the skin and tidy up any debris.

The Israelites found blood essential for their lives in another way. As God prepared to send the death angel throughout the land of Egypt, He instructed the Israelites to place the blood of a sacrificed lamb on the doorposts and lintel of their homes. Whoever failed to do that found their first-born stuck dead by morning.

Blood is just as essential for spiritual life

as it is for physical life. It is the blood of Jesus Christ that paid for our sins, making it possible for us to be reunited with the Father (Heb. 9:12-14). Furthermore, it is the blood of Christ that continues to take away the penalty for our sins so that we can have fellowship with God and with man (Heb. 10:19-22, 1 John 1:7). Without the blood of God's Perfect Lamb—Jesus Christ—we would be unable to experience forgiveness for sin and the joys of the Christian life.

When you come before God the Father, plead the blood of Christ. It is not by your own effort but by His blood that you are saved. Furthermore, as you daily confess your sins, claim the cleansing power of Christ's blood to wash you clean. His blood keeps on cleansing us from sin. The solution to sin—past, present and future—is found in His blood.

Before we can be made white as snow, we must first be washed red with Christ's blood.

Reflections/Prayer Requests

_____

_____

_____

DAY 25

Exodus 12:30-32

So Pharaoh rose in the night,
he, all his servants, and all the Egyptians;
and there was a great cry in Egypt, for there
was not a house where there was not one
dead. Then he called for Moses and Aaron by
night, and said, "Rise, go out from among my
people, both you and the children of Israel.
And go, serve the LORD as you have said.
Also take your flocks and your herds,
as you have said, and be gone;
and bless me also."

Pay Attention!

There's an old story about a man who bought a mule from a farmer. A few days later he brought it back and said, "I can't get this beast to do a thing." "That's strange," the farmer replied, "I never had any problems with him. Let's see if he will obey me."

The farmer then walked over, picked up a two by four and hit the mule over the head. "What did you do that for?" the man exclaimed. "Well," said the farmer, "the first thing you have to do is get his attention."

That's apparently what it took for Pharaoh. Nine times God used quieter and gentler means to get his attention, but to no avail. Only the extreme experience of losing his firstborn child pierced this arrogant ruler's hardened heart and got him to do what he should have done in the first place.

God doesn't like to deal in extremes. His first choice is always the "still, small voice." Only when forced by the wickedness and stubbornness of an unrepentant heart will He resort to drastic measures. Yet that in itself is a sign of His love. Where others give up, God loves us so much that He is even willing to hurt us if that's what it takes to reach us.

Are you putting God in a position where He has to use drastic measures to get you to listen? There's a better way. Hear His still, small voice and you won't ever have to feel His "two by four."

If you don't listen to God's whisper, you'll surely hear His shout.

Reflections/Prayer Requests

DAY 26

Exodus 12:31, 33

*Then he called for
Moses and Aaron by night, and said,
"Rise, go out from among my people,
both you and the children of Israel. And go,
serve the LORD as you have said. . . .*

*And the Egyptians urged the people,
that they might send them out of
the land in haste. For they said,
"We shall all be dead."*

Persona Non Grata

Countries have a category for people whom they will not allow to enter their borders or whom they encourage to leave as soon as possible. These people are classified as *persona non grata*. Literally it means "your person is not welcome."

Through plagues of blood, gnats, hailstones and much more, the Egyptians had stubbornly refused to let the Israelites go. But the death of all the firstborn in Egypt turned the tide. Instead of being a "natural resource" to be held as slaves, God's people became *persona non grata*. The Egyptians couldn't get rid of them fast enough! Pharaoh didn't even wait for morning but called Moses and Aaron at night, and his subjects "urged the people, that they might send them out of the land in haste."

When the time is right, God can accomplish a lot in a hurry. As God works to carry out His purposes, the time may seem to drag on. But when God's goal is reached, events quickly fall into place.

That's why it is so important for us to be ready. Like the Israelites who had their clothes packed and their food made, we need to be set to go at a moment's notice. In a short period of time—even the twinkling of an eye—we can become *persona non grata* to earth and on our way to a better place. Don't be caught unprepared.

If you feel unwelcome on earth, remember that you are accepted in heaven.

Reflections/Prayer Requests

_____

_____

_____

_____

_____

_____

_____

DAY 27

Exodus 12:43-45

*And the LORD said to Moses and Aaron,
"This is the ordinance of the Passover:
No foreigner shall eat it. But every man's
servant who is bought for money,
when you have circumcised him,
then he may eat it.
A sojourner and a hired servant
shall not eat it."*

Family Only

I have spent a lot of money feeding my
family, providing clothing and shelter for
them, paying college tuition, even offering
opportunities for them to enjoy themselves.
I haven't minded doing that—after all, they
are my family! But unless there were exten-
uating circumstances, I would not have
been so joyful about doing that for someone who did not belong to my family. Some
privileges are for family members only.

That's the way God felt about the
Passover. It was a celebration for His family. As children of Abraham, the Jews were
given the right to look to God as their
Father, and the Passover was for them.
Those just passing through (sojourners)
and those who were paid to be part of the
group (hired servants) were not family
members and therefore were not eligible to

enjoy family privileges.

In the church age, we also have a family-only celebration—the Lord's Supper. This service is modeled after the Passover feast. As Passover reminds the Jews of their deliverance from bondage in Egypt, Communion reminds Christians of their deliverance from the bondage of sin, which Christ provided through His death on the cross. To participate in this service, one must be a member of the family, and the only way to become a part of the family is to receive Christ as Savior.

The next time you prepare to partake in the Communion service, ask yourself, "Have I become part of God's family? Have I trusted Jesus Christ as my Savior? Am I a member in good standing by confessing my sins?" If the answers to these questions are yes, do what the Israelites did. Celebrate your freedom. Enjoy being a member of the family.

Family privileges are for members only.

Reflections/Prayer Requests

_____

_____

_____

_____

DAY 28

Exodus 13:1-2

*Then the LORD spoke to Moses, saying,
"Consecrate to Me all the firstborn, whatever
opens the womb among the
children of Israel, both of man
and beast; it is Mine."*

An Issue of Ownership

A little boy told a friend that his father had bought him a new ball. "What's it like?" his friend wanted to know. "Well, it's big and round," the young boy said. "What else?" his friend inquired. "It's yellow with blue stripes," the boy responded. "What else?" the friend continued. After a moment of thought, the boy came up with the most special characteristic of all. "It's mine!"

God made it very clear to Moses that every firstborn child of man or beast belonged to Him. He said, "It's Mine." In one sense, everything belongs to God by right of creation. But He laid claim to these firstborn children by right of redemption. Because God brought the people out of the land of Egypt, the firstfruits of their loins and their livestock was to be set aside as His special property.

Jesus Christ also lays claim to those whom He has redeemed. The apostle Paul told Titus that it was Christ "who gave Himself for us, that He might redeem us from every lawless deed and purify for Himself His own special people, zealous for good works" (Titus 2:14).

As Jesus' special purchase, delivered out of the slave market of sin, you are the most precious thing in God's creation. But this also gives you a special responsibility. Paul says, "For you were bought at a price; therefore glorify God in your body and in your spirit, which are God's" (1 Cor. 6:20). Have you settled the ownership issue in your life? The Bible says you don't belong to yourself. Christ bought you and He wants you to be His special possession. Remember whom you belong to and give Him joy in all you do today.

You are special not because of what you own, but because of Who owns you.

Reflections/Prayer Requests

DAY 29

Exodus 13:18

Then it came to pass, when Pharaoh had let the people go, that God did not lead them by way of the land of the Philistines, although that was near; for God said, "Lest perhaps the people change their minds when they see war, and return to Egypt."

War No More

The pastor of a small southern church was on his way home when he met an acquaintance from town who was not a member of his church. After chatting for a while the man asked the pastor how many members he had. The pastor responded, "I have fifty active members." His friend replied, "My, that certainly speaks well for you." But the preacher responded, "Well, I wouldn't say that. All fifty are active—but twenty-five are actively working for me and the other twenty-five are actively working against me!" Too frequently that's an accurate description of the church.

When God brought His people out of Egypt, He made a special effort to avoid places where strife would likely occur. He knew such belligerent encounters would discourage His people and perhaps even cause them to return to their bondage in Egypt. God was willing to go the long way around rather than risk a hurtful battle, even though He could have won.

Strife within the church never accomplishes anything positive. Invariably, innocent people get hurt. It is absolutely necessary that we never compromise the basic truths of the faith, but issues such as choir robes versus casual dress, hymnals versus an overhead projector, or a later service versus an earlier service ought never cause resentment among believers.

Are you "at war" with anyone in the church? Are you allowing minor issues or personality conflicts to undermine the unity of the faith? Jesus Christ died to bring unity. Make sure you're not the cause of disunity. God's Word says, "If it is possible, as much as depends on you, live peaceably with all men" (Rom. 12:18). It's much more possible than most of us want to admit.

Until we recognize who the real enemy is, we won't know who our friends are.

Reflections/Prayer Requests

_____

_____

_____

_____

DAY 30

Exodus 13:19

*And Moses took the bones of
Joseph with him, for he had placed the
children of Israel under solemn oath, saying,
"God will surely visit you, and you shall
carry up my bones from here with you."*

Forget Me Not

Most of us forget much quicker than we remember. It's easy to identify with the person who said, "I write down everything I want to recollect. That way, instead of spending a lot of time trying to recall what I wrote down, I spend the time looking for the paper I wrote it on."

As Moses and the Israelites prepared to leave Egypt, they exhumed the remains of Joseph and took them along. These bones were a reminder of Joseph's faith. It was his trust in God's future deliverance that prompted him to make his kinsmen swear they would not leave his bones behind. Such faith is worthy to be remembered.

While we don't want to fixate on the past, we don't want to forget it either. We can learn valuable lessons from remembering the way God worked in the lives of His saints who preceded us. They remind us, for example, of God's faithfulness. We find encouragement for our own struggles when we see the steadfast love He demonstrated toward them. They also remind us of God's holiness. When our spiritual ancestors disobeyed God, they faced His holy correction.

Is there someone from your family who needs to be remembered? Perhaps you know some elderly saint, homebound or restricted to a nursing home, who could bless your life by his or her memories. Before your days all become the past, take some time to remember the past. It may be one of the greater blessings of your present.

We cannot relive the past, so let's make sure we remember it.

Reflections/Prayer Requests

_____

_____

_____

_____

_____

_____

_____

DAY 31

Compass in the Sky

Scientists have developed what is called a Global Positioning System, which consists of 24 satellites circling the earth at six different levels. No matter where we might be in the world, at least five of those satellites should be available to track our position. By using special equipment to bounce signals off these orbiting signposts, we can pinpoint where we are day or night within 100 meters. With the GPS we never have to worry about being lost.

As the Israelites set out into unknown territory, God also provided them with a Global Positioning System. In the daytime it was a pillar of a cloud and at night it was a pillar of fire. God's people never had to worry about getting lost so long as they paid attention to these celestial guides.

Although we no longer have the pillars of

cloud or fire, God still has given a compass to guide His people. We call it the Bible. No matter where we live, the universal truths of God's Word are able to pinpoint where we are in our spiritual journey. Furthermore, if we will apply these truths to our lives, Scripture always will lead us to where we need to be. We never need to wander aimlessly. If we pay attention to God's Word, we will never get lost.

Always remember, however, that the Bible is effective only if we read it. If we keep it on the shelf or let it lie on the coffee table, it can't provide the guidance we need to find our way. Why not spend at least 15 minutes a day reading and meditating on this vital compass for your life? Used appropriately, God's Word will make sure you never get lost.

God's Word always points in the right direction.

Reflections/Prayer Requests

_____

_____

_____

_____

_____